JEWELRY CRAFTS

Barrie Caldecott

Consultant: Henry Pluckrose

Photography: Chris Fairclough

FRANKLIN WATTS
New York/London/Toronto/Sydney

Copyright © 1991 Franklin Watts

Franklin Watts
387 Park Avenue South
New York, NY 10016

Library of Congress Cataloging-in-Publication Data
Caldecott, Barrie.
    Jewelry crafts / by Barrie Caldecott.
        p.   cm. — (Fresh start)
    Includes index.
    Summary: Provides step-by-step instructions for making jewelry
using readily available materials.
    ISBN 0-531-14203-5
    1. Jewelry making—Juvenile literature.   1. Jewelry making.
2. Handicraft.]   I. Title.   II. Series: Fresh start (London,
England)
TT212.C33   1992
745.594'2—dc20   91-9887
                                                                 CIP AC

Design: K and Co.

Editor: Jenny Wood

Typeset by Lineage Ltd,
Watford, England

Printed in Belgium

Contents

This book describes activities which use the following:

Acetate (0.175mm thick, 4 colors)
Adhesive tape (5 colors)
Aluminum foil
Beads – wood, glass or plastic, various sizes and quantities – see activities for details – 1 pearl bead, 10mm diameter
Bowl
Broach-tipped bradawl
Candle holders (4, of the flower type used on birthday cakes)
Candy wrappers
Cardboard
Compass
Cookie sheet (old)
Craft knife
Cutting board
Double-sided tape (½in wide)
Drinking straws (straight and bendable, in a variety of colors)
Duco cement ®
Earring clips and/or hooks
Egg
Egg cup
Embroidery thread cotton, (3 colors)
Eyelet punch
Eyelets (for ¼in hole)
Feathers (fluffy)
Felt-tip pens
Garden wire (plastic-coated)
Gold lurex braid (¼in wide flat strip)
Hole punch
Knitting needle (no. 11)
Masking tape

Mixing stick
Modeling or cutting board (plastic-coated)
Modeling material – such as Formello, or Miracle Clay, such as Della Robbia
Newspaper
Ornamental glass stone (cabochon)
Oven (you will need access to an oven in order to bake the modeling material. ASK AN ADULT FOR HELP.)
Paint (gold enamel)
Paintbrush
Paper – drawing paper in 5 different colors – 1 sheet of drawing paper, 3in x 29in – graph paper
Paper clips (plastic-coated, various colors)
Pencil
Pin clip (for brooch)
Plastic tubing (clear, 6mm and 10mm outside diameter)
Pliers
Rhinestones (2mm and 5mm diameter, see pages 42 and 46 for details)
Rhinestone strip (3mm wide)
Rolling pin
Round-nosed pliers
Ruler
Scissors
Silver gift-wrapping tape
Sticky dots
Tape (clear)
Tissues
Water pipe insulating foam (1½in outside diameter, for ½in diameter water pipe)
Wire cutters
UHU glue (or similar)

People wear more jewelry today than they have ever worn before. Shopping centers abound with jewelry and gift shops selling the traditionally accepted gold, silver and diamond rings, and necklaces and earrings and costume jewelry commonly associated with the craft. But individual designer-craftspeople, who sell their work in craft shops, galleries and by commission are, through their use of colorful and inexpensive materials, breaking down the traditional restrictions imposed by precious metals and stones. It is the design of this "nontraditional" type of jewelry that this book explores.

Some hints

A table covered with a protective layer of newspaper and a cutting board will make a good work surface for the activities presented in this book.

The majority of the materials listed are readily available from stationers and/or artists' materials stores. You will find information on how to obtain any special materials (such as beads, rhinestones and feathers) on page 46.

In addition to the usual craft tools of scissors, ruler and a craft knife, you will need others such as pliers, wire cutters, round-nosed pliers and a bradawl with broach tip. You may be able to obtain these from an adult's household tool kit (ask permission first!), or see page 46 for advice on where to purchase them.

On your own

Once you have completed the activities in the book, follow the technique demonstrated for each design to make a variety of pieces for yourself. You may even find that you are inspired to invent new designs of your own!

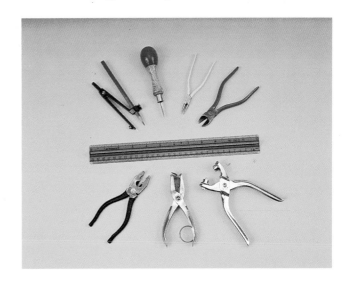

1 Some of the tools you will need to make your own jewelry pieces.

Plastic bracelet and necklace

These simply made pieces use clear plastic tubing as their basis.

You will need clear plastic tubing (¼in and ½in outside diameter), felt-tip pens, scissors, a craft knife, a ruler, a modeling or cutting board (plastic-coated), Miracle Clay or Formello, aluminum foil, an old cookie sheet, tissues, masking tape, a knitting needle (no. 11) and tape (clear). You will also need access to an oven, which you should preheat according to the modeling material instructions.

HINT: BEFORE USING THE MODELING MATERIAL, ALWAYS ROLL IT IN YOUR HANDS TO SOFTEN IT.

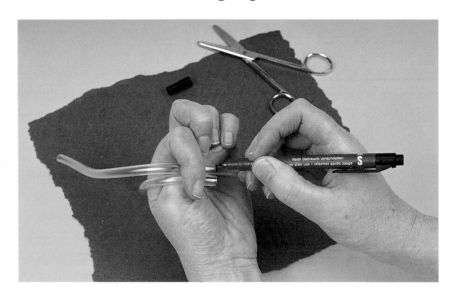

1 Shape your hand as if about to slide a bracelet onto your wrist. Wrap the ¼in diameter tubing around your knuckles and mark the point where the ends meet. Cut off the length at the mark.

2 On your modeling board, roll out a piece of modeling material into a rod approximately 2½in long. The tapered ends should just fit into the tube.

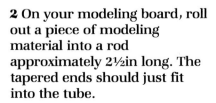

3 Bend the modeling material to form the same curve as that of the tube when the ends are held together. Line the cookie sheet with a piece of aluminum foil, and lay the modeling material on top.

ASK AN ADULT TO HELP YOU PLACE THE SHEET IN THE OVEN. Bake the modeling material according to directions on the package. Remove, and allow the modeling material to cool and harden.

4 Roll up a tissue and cut it into approximately twenty-five pieces, each ½in long. (The exact number of pieces you need will depend on the length of your tube.) Color the pieces with felt-tip pens.

5 Wind a 2in length of masking tape around the end of the knitting needle to make a ramrod. Roll the pieces of colored tissue into small lengths and use the knitting needle to push them into the tube. Work from both ends until the tube is nearly full, leaving ½in at each end empty.

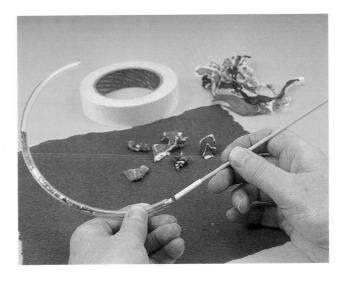

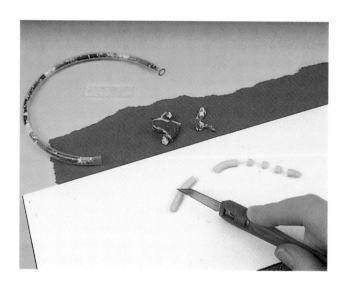

6 Lay the hardened modeling material on your board, and use the craft knife to cut off the tapered ends. Make a jointing piece by cutting a ¾in length. Cut an extra jointing piece and some shorter ¼in lengths. Use these shorter lengths as "spacers" in other bangle bracelets you experiment with later (see page 9).

7 Push the jointing piece halfway into one end of the tube and bring the other end around to join the bracelet together. (If the jointing piece is loose, hold the ends together with tape.)

8 Follow exactly the same procedure to make the matching necklace. This time, however, use the ½in diameter plastic tubing, and cut it to a length long enough to go over your head.

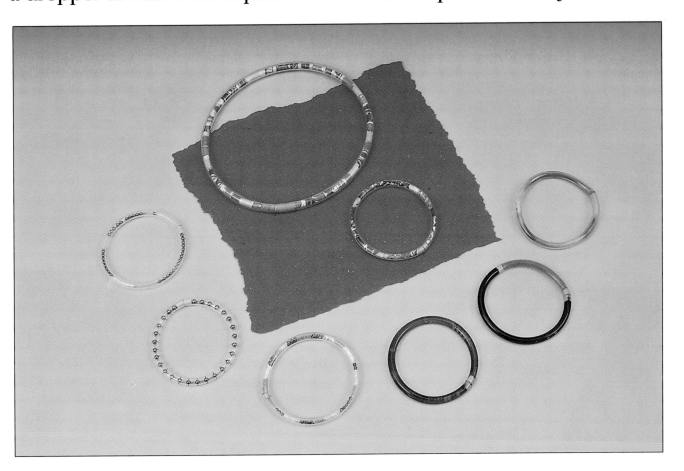

Try making your own bracelets and necklaces, using different "fillings". Here are some ideas:

1 Loosely fitting ball bearings, with spacers.

2 Tightly fitting ball bearings pushed into place with a knitting needle.

3 Seeds.

4 Colored water and beads. (Use a dropper to insert the liquid into the tube.)

5 Different-colored waters, with spacers.

(For suggestions 4 and 5, make sure that the jointing pieces fit tightly, but use washable colors in case of leakage.)

6 Powder paint. (Use a small paper funnel to put the powder into the tube.)

Now experiment for yourself.

9 Experiment with other "fillings" to make plastic bracelets and necklaces of your own.

Pendant necklace with beads

You will need metallic candy wrappers (four different colors, if possible), a pencil, a ruler, scissors, double-sided tape (½in wide), drinking straws, plastic-coated garden wire, wire cutters, round-nosed pliers, twenty round wooden or glass beads, stranded embroidery thread (three different colors) and masking tape.

1 Cut four strips of metallic paper from your candy wrappers (one in each color, if possible). Each strip should be ½in wide.

2 Cut a 2½in length of double-sided tape. Attach the strips of metallic paper to the sticky side of the tape, as shown.

3 Turn the tape over and cut off the excess metallic paper.

4 Cut diagonally across the tape to form two triangles.

5 Peel the backing off the double-sided tape at the wide end of one triangle. Attach the triangle to a drinking straw so that the point of the triangle sticks out at right angles to the straw. Remove the rest of the backing and roll the tape around the straw to form a bead.

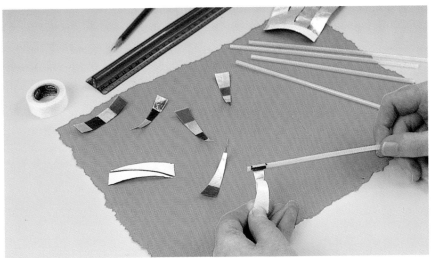

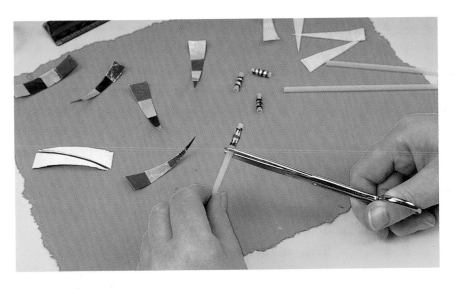

6 Cut the bead from the straw, leaving 2mm of straw on either side of the metallic paper. Make another bead from the second triangle, then make twenty-one more beads in the same way. Vary the order in which you attach the strips of metallic paper to the tape (see picture **2**), so that your beads have different color patterns.

7 Cut a piece of garden wire 5in long. Straighten it, then bend a loop in one end using the round-nosed pliers.

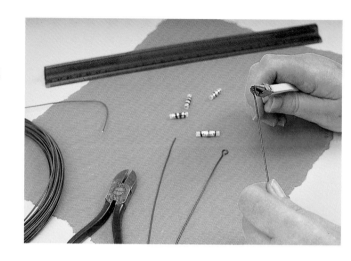

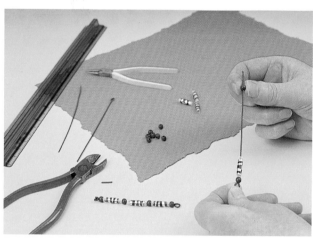

8 Slide a wooden or glass bead onto the wire, then add a handmade bead. Repeat this pattern twice, then add another wooden or glass bead. Cut off the wire so that ½in is left. Make a loop in the wire to hold the beads in place. Make four more lengths of beads in the same way.

9 Cut three equal lengths of embroidery thread (one of each color). (The length you cut should be equal to the measurement one and a half times around your head.) Catch the top ends together with masking tape, tape down onto your work surface and braid the strands. Tape the bottom ends together when you have finished.

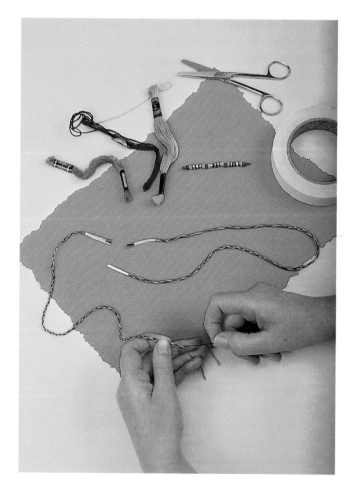

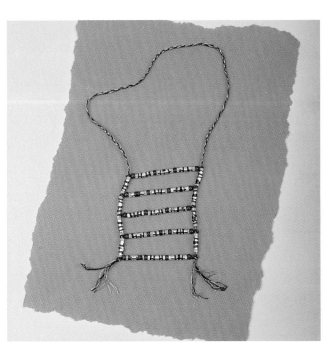

10 Thread the braid through the wire loops in the lengths of beads, using the spare handmade beads as spacers between each wire. Tie the ends of the braid to the last wire loop on each side of the necklace and remove the masking tape. Pull the individual strands apart to form tassels.

11 Experiment with different colors of metallic paper and arrangements of beads.

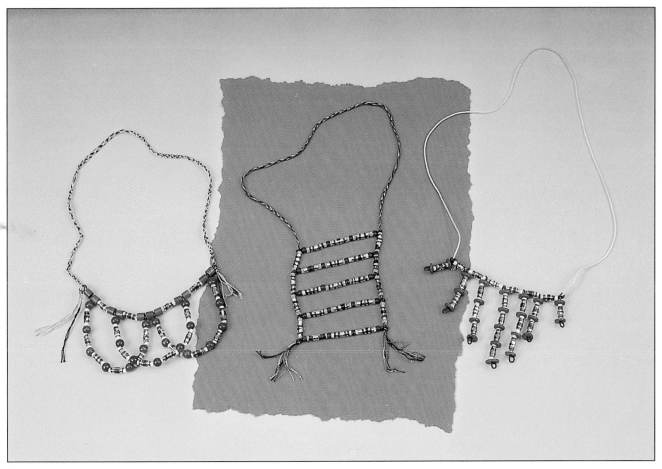

Ornamental glass stone ring

To make a ring fit your finger, you need to make a simple tapered mandrel or ring triblet. This will enable you to make rings for a wide variety of finger sizes.

You will need a sheet of drawing paper 3in x 29in, a pencil, masking tape, scissors, three colors of Formello or Miracle Clay, which you can glaze, a ruler, a craft knife, a modeling or cutting board (plastic-coated), aluminum foil, an ornamental glass stone (cabochon) and an old cookie sheet. You will also need access to an oven, which you should preheat according to the modeling material instructions. This ring is made with three different colors of modeling material rolled into a multicolored spiral, but you can use a single color if you prefer.

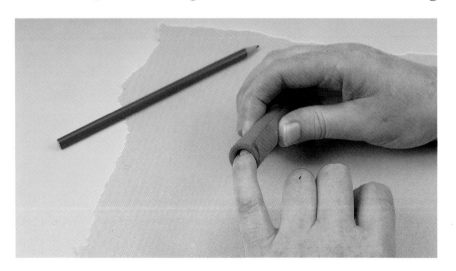

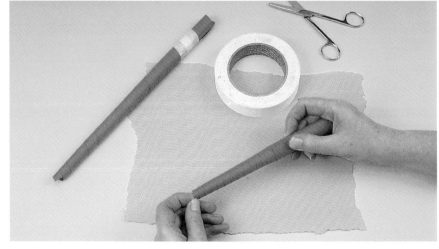

1 Roll the sheet of drawing paper around the pencil. Remove the pencil and, holding the outside of the coil, let the paper spring apart until you can put the end of your little finger into the hole.

2 Holding the tube tightly, push the middle of the coil out to form the tapered mandrel. Wrap masking tape around the fat end to keep it from unwinding.

3 Decide on which finger you want to wear the ring and hold the mandrel against it. Mark with a pencil the place where you can see the mandrel on either side of the ring position on your finger.

4 Cut three equal-sized pieces of modeling material (one of each color) and lay them on your modeling board. Using the palm of your hand, roll out each piece into a long, thin rod approximately 5in long x ⅛in diameter.

5 Lay the three rods together and roll them into one rod. Put a twist in the rod by rolling it away from you with your right hand and towards you with your left. The rod should double in length, be about ¼in in diameter in the middle, and taper into points at the ends.

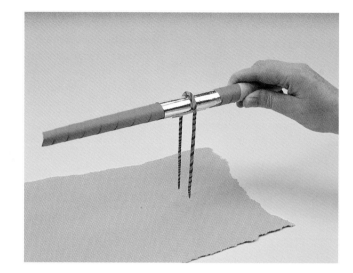

6 Wrap a piece of aluminum foil around the mandrel at the point where you marked it with a pencil, and tape into position. Hang the rod over the foil. Make sure that the ends hanging down are the same length. (If necessary, adjust by rotating the mandrel until the lengths are equal.)

7 Wrap each end of the rod once around the mandrel. Gently press the ornamental stone on to the top of the rod, as shown.

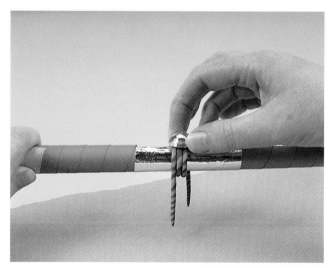

8 Bring the loose ends up and wrap them around the stone. Gently press them in.

9 Tape the mandrel (with the ring still in position) upright across the cookie sheet. ASK AN ADULT TO HELP YOU PLACE THE SHEET IN THE OVEN. Bake the modeling material according to the package's instructions. Remove, and allow the modeling material to cool and harden.

10 You can also make rings using marbles, shells and stones. Experiment with other colors of modeling material and other "jewels."

Wire earrings

Plastic-coated wire paper clips are the basis of these colorful earrings. Earring clips or hooks will have to be chosen to suit your needs (see picture 9).

You will need plastic-coated paper clips (various colors), pliers, wire cutters, 124 wooden, glass or plastic beads (a size that will slide onto the paper clip wire), UHU (or similar adhesive) and earring mounts to suit, with an attachment for a loop of wire.

1 Carefully open out and straighten a blue paper clip into the shape shown on the right of the picture. Use the pliers if necessary. The long, straight piece of wire is formed from the outer part of the paper clip and the first bend. The two remaining bends in the paper clip are opened to form right angles.

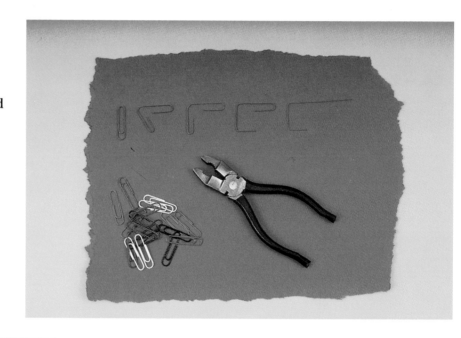

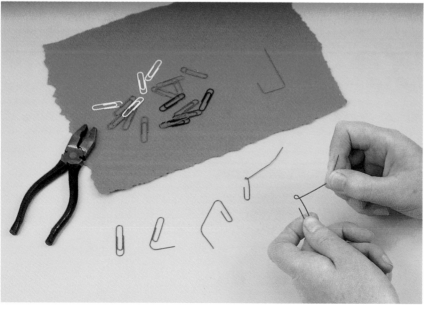

2 Straighten the outside loop of a red paper clip. Bend the next loop up tightly until the hole it creates fits loosely on the wire of the blue paper clip.

3 Using the wire cutters, carefully cut off the bent part of the wire at the loop, as shown. Press the loop flat with the pliers. Cut off the spare wire 1in from the loop. Make four more red wires and five yellow wires in this way. Each yellow wire should be 1½in long.

4 Slide five beads onto each wire, as shown. Glue the last bead in place on each wire.

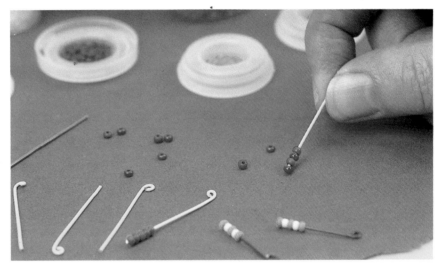

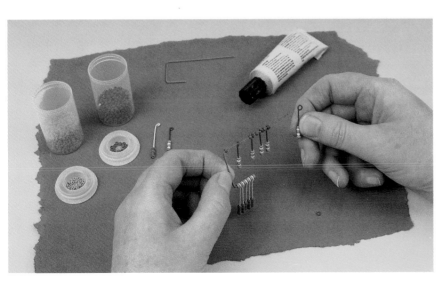

5 Thread the yellow wire loops onto the short end of the blue paper clip, with a bead at either end and one between each loop. Put glue on the ends of each bead to hold them in position. Now thread the red wire loops onto the long end of the blue paper clip. Place a bead at each end and one between each loop. Glue the end beads in place.

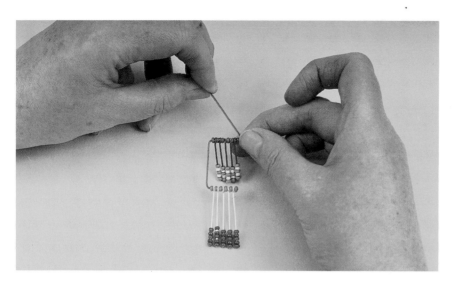

6 Bend up the long end of the blue paper clip to trap the top row of loops, as shown.

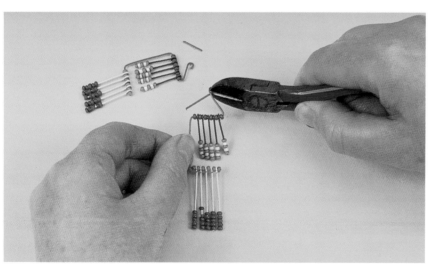

7 Bend a loop in the wire, as shown, over the middle of the rows. Use the wire cutters to cut off the spare wire past the loop, and leave the loop slightly open.

8 Attach an earring clip or hook to the loop, then close the loop using the pliers. Make another earring in exactly the same way.

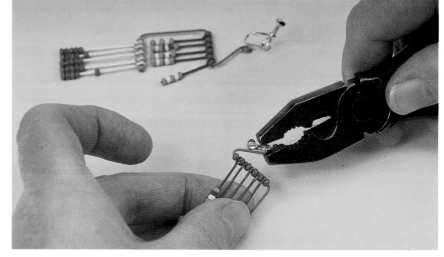

9 Use other colors and shapes to make a whole range of earrings. Here are some ideas. The picture also shows different types of earring clips and hooks.

Paper necklace

A simple arrangement of paper cones on a length of garden wire is the basis for this colorful necklace. A cardboard pattern is used to make the cutting out of the repeated shapes easier.

You will need a piece of cardboard (approximately 3in x 3in), a compass, a pencil, a ruler, scissors, colored paper (five different colors), double-sided tape, plastic-coated garden wire, wire cutters, one large wooden bead, thirty-eight flat wooden beads (approximately ½in in diameter), drinking straws and round-nosed pliers.

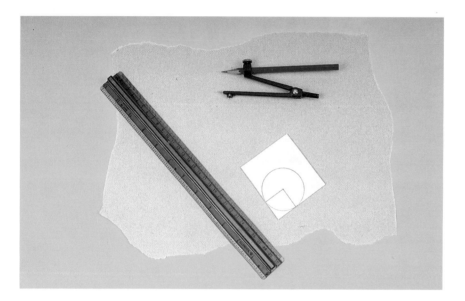

1 To make the pattern, draw a circle on the piece of cardboard. The radius should be 1in, and the edge of the circle should touch the cardboard on two sides. Draw a square from the center of the circle, as shown.

2 Cut out the square, then the rest of the circle shape, as shown. The circle with cut-out wedge will be your pattern. Measure ¾in around the edge of the circle from one end of the cut-out wedge and mark a dot. Draw a line from the center of the circle to this dot.

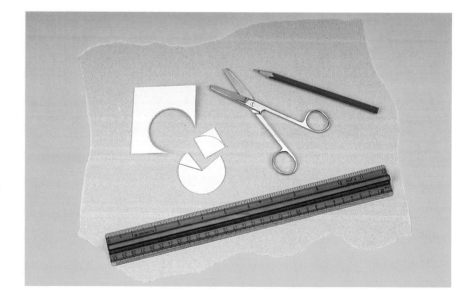

3 Cut out eighteen pieces of colored paper, using the pattern as a guide. You will need four pieces of each of four colors, and two pieces of the fifth color.

4 Place the pattern over each paper shape, and mark a dot where the penciled line on the pattern meets the edge of the cut-out shape.

5 Stick a piece of double-sided tape from the center of each paper shape to the dot on its edge. Trim off the excess tape.

6 To make the cones, peel the backing from the tape and bring the other side of the wedge over until it reaches the penciled dot. Press firmly to stick down.

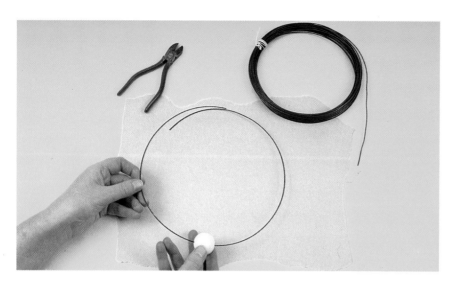

7 Cut off a 29in length of garden wire and thread the large bead onto it.

8 Cut a tiny piece off the pointed end of each paper cone, to create a small hole. Thread the cones onto the wire, with a flat bead after each one to act as a spacer. Arrange the colors as shown, or choose your own design. Sequins ½in in diameter could be used as spacers instead of beads, but you may have to make the holes in the sequins larger to fit them onto the wire.

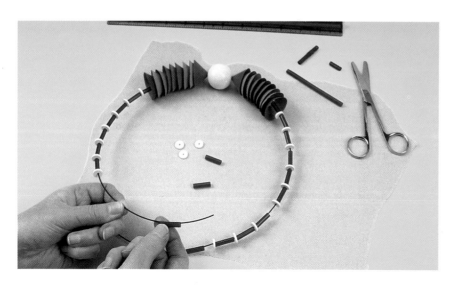

9 Cut twenty lengths of drinking straw, each ¾in long, and thread them alternately with more flat beads on each side of the paper cones. Cut the remaining wire to leave 1½in sticking out at each end.

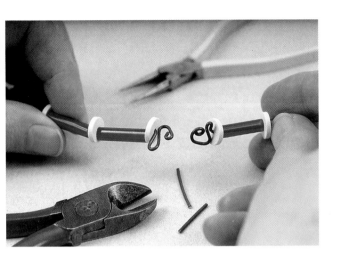

10 Using the round-nosed pliers, bend a small loop in each of the wire ends to make them safe. Then bend the wire back and forth to trap the last beads on the necklace.

11 Bend a hook in one wire end, and a loop in the other, to form a catch.

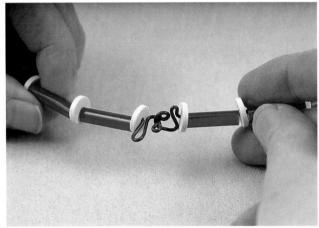

12 Use different colors and arrangements of cones to design a variety of necklaces.

Brooch and earrings

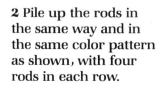

The brooch and earrings shown here make use of the colorful properties of the modeling material described on page 6. Rhinestones ("glass diamonds") are used to give a bright, sparkling finish to the pieces.

You will need modeling material (five colors – green, yellow, purple, red and black), a modeling or cutting board (plastic-coated), a ruler, a rolling pin, a craft knife, two pieces of stiff cardboard (each 4in x 2in), aluminum foil, an old cookie sheet, Duco cement®, a mixing stick, two earring clips, a pin clip, rhinestones (thirty-two 2mm diameter, and three 5mm diameter), UHU (or similar adhesive), felt-tip pens and graph paper. You will also need access to an oven, which you should preheat according to the modeling material instructions.

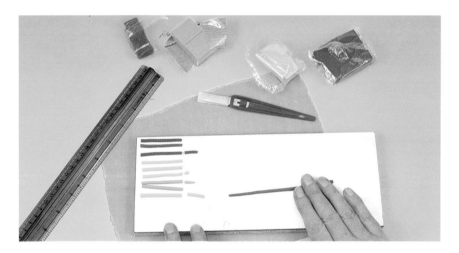

1 Lay pieces of modeling material on the modeling board, then, using the palm of your hand, roll each piece into a rod 2in long and ¼in in diameter. You will need two green, four yellow, four purple and six red rods.

2 Pile up the rods in the same way and in the same color pattern as shown, with four rods in each row.

3 Use the rolling pin to squeeze the rods gently together until they form a solid, square-sectioned block. Trim off the uneven ends with the craft knife.

4 Press some black modeling material between your fingers to form a thin sheet. Roll it flat with the rolling pin, turning it over frequently to prevent it from sticking to the board. Cut out a strip and wrap it around the solid block.

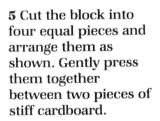

5 Cut the block into four equal pieces and arrange them as shown. Gently press them together between two pieces of stiff cardboard.

6 Carefully slice through the pressed block (as you would slice a loaf of bread), to give you two pieces of equal thickness. Roll out one piece until it is about ⅛in thick. Roll it alternately at right angles to keep it square. Turn it over frequently to prevent it from sticking to the board. This piece is the base of your brooch.

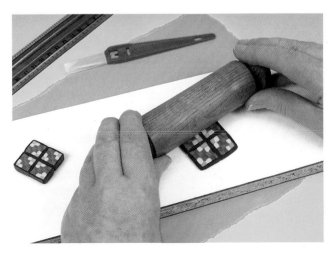

7 Using a piece of stiff cardboard, press the second half of the pressed block on the black sides to make it smaller and wider. Rotate it between presses, to keep the square shape. Continue until the block is reduced to about ¾in square.

8 Slice off the ends. Cut the rest into ⅛in pieces to make the earrings and buttons (see picture **9**). Place these and the brooch on an aluminum foil-lined cookie sheet. ASK AN ADULT TO HELP YOU PLACE THE SHEET IN THE OVEN. Bake the modeling material according to the package instructions. Remove, and allow to cool and harden.

9 On a piece of cardboard, put a small quantity of Duco cement®. Follow the instructions given on the tube. ASK AN ADULT TO HELP YOU WITH THIS. Place a blob of cement on each earring clip, then press each clip onto one of the earring pieces. Do the same with the pin clip and attach this to the brooch. Allow the cement to harden. (Spare earring squares can be drilled – ASK AN ADULT TO HELP YOU WITH THIS – to form colorful matching buttons.)

10 Decorate the earrings and brooch with the rhinestones, as shown. Use a rod of modeling material to pick up the rhinestones and apply glue to the back to glue them in position.

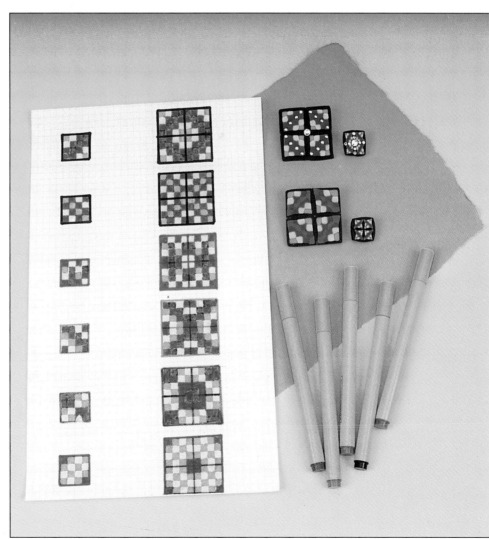

11 You can arrange the rods in many different ways. Experiment on graph paper using felt-tip pens first, until you find a design you like. Here are some ideas.

Foam bangle

This large bangle uses water pipe insulating foam which is light and flexible. Any color of foam will do, as the main colors of the bangle are created by the addition of adhesive tapes and sticky dots. A simple pattern is used to make the sides and angles of this bold piece equal.

You will need a piece of cardboard (4in x 5in), a ruler, a pencil, a craft knife, scissors, 3 feet of water pipe insulating foam (1½in outside diameter, for a ½in diameter water pipe), UHU (or similar adhesive), adhesive tape (five colors), silver gift wrapping tape, double-sided tape, sticky dots (white or colored) and felt-tip pens.

1 To make a pattern for cutting the foam at 45°, divide the 4in side of the cardboard into three equal 1½in parts, and the 5in side into three parts: 1½in, 2in and 1½in. Draw pencil lines to divide the cardboard into sections, and draw diagonal lines across the corner squares, as shown.

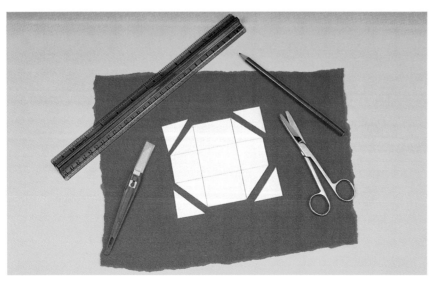

2 Score the two 5in lines with the craft knife. Cut off the corners of the squares along the diagonals.

3 Fold the cardboard at right angles along the scored lines and place the foam inside. Using this cardboard pattern as a guide, carefully cut through each end of the foam with the craft knife. This piece is the first side of the bangle.

4 Line up the cut end of the foam with the pattern. Now cut through the other end to make the next side of the bangle. Repeat until you have four identical pieces of foam.

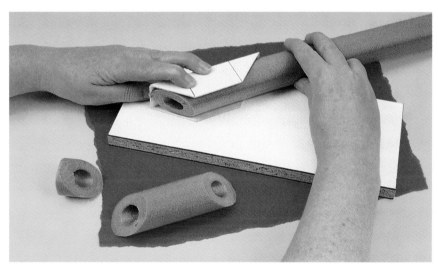

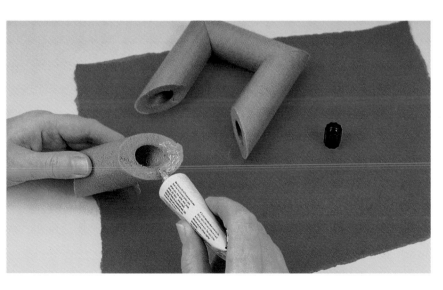

5 Spread glue evenly over each end of the foam tubes and press them together in a square to form the bangle.

6 Wrap one color of tape around the outside edge of the bangle. Pull it tight as you stick it to the foam.

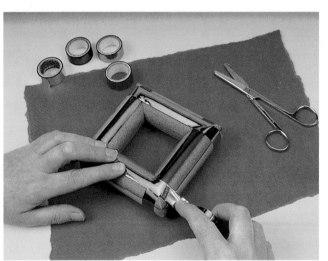

7 Wrap different colored tapes along each section of the bangle, overlapping at the corners.

8 Divide the inside edge of each side of the bangle into five equal parts. Cut twenty strips of silver tape, each 5in long, and apply ¼in of double-sided tape to each end of each strip. Stick five strips to each side of the bangle, as shown.

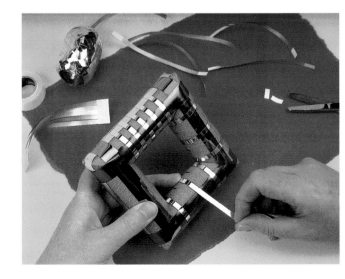

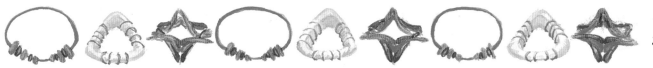

9 Color some sticky dots with felt-tip pens (or use ready-colored sticky dots). Stick these to the places where the colored tapes cross and where the silver tape crosses the outside edge tape.

10 You can achieve many different effects by applying a variety of colors and tapes. Make different shapes by changing the angle on the pattern to 30° for a three-sided bangle, or 54° for a five-sided bangle. Try to make a round bangle by cutting and joining very small wedges.

A simple arrangement of colored, bendable drinking straws provides the structure for this flamboyant necklace. Bought feathers are used here but it is worth making a collection of any you find outdoors, as they are easily colored using inks.

You will need bendable drinking straws (two colors, approximately twelve of each color), scissors, adhesive tape (colored), a ruler, UHU (or similar adhesive), fluffy feathers and masking tape.

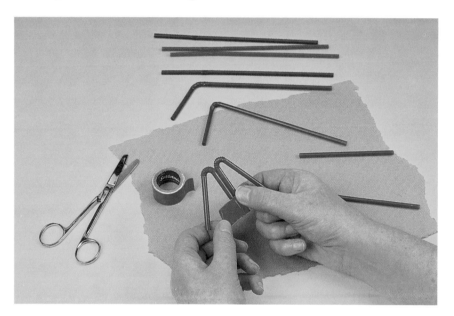

1 Take a blue straw and pull apart the accordion section so that it bends around and back on itself. Do the same with another blue straw. Tape the two straws together as shown. Cut the long ends on each straw so that all the lengths are equal.

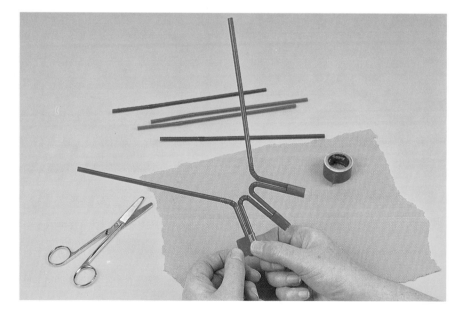

2 Take two full-length blue straws and tape the short ends to each side of the piece you have just made.

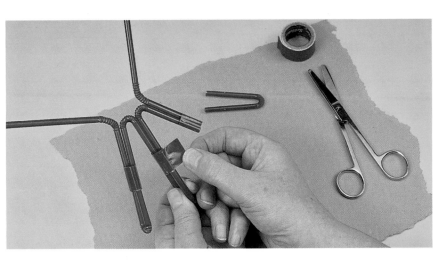

3 Bend, cut and tape three more blue straws, as shown, joining each to one of the taped "prongs" on the piece you have just made.

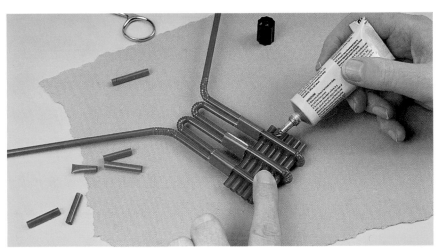

4 Cut three pieces, each 2½in long, from the straight part of a blue straw. Cut three 2½in lengths from a red straw. Push these lengths between the folded blue straws on the bottom part of the main piece until there is no space left. The last straw length should fit tightly. Now glue the straw lengths into position.

5 Cut a red straw as shown in picture **1**, then cut a straight 2¾in length of blue straw. Join the blue straw to the red straw by making a ½in slit in the end of each straw. Slide the straws into each other and wrap tape over the joint to keep the straws in position.

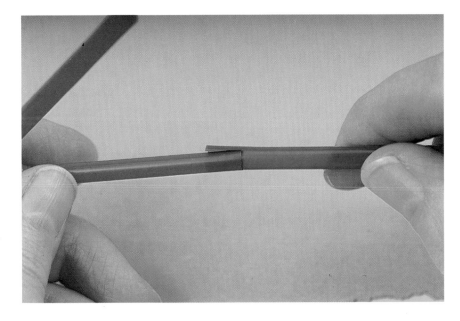

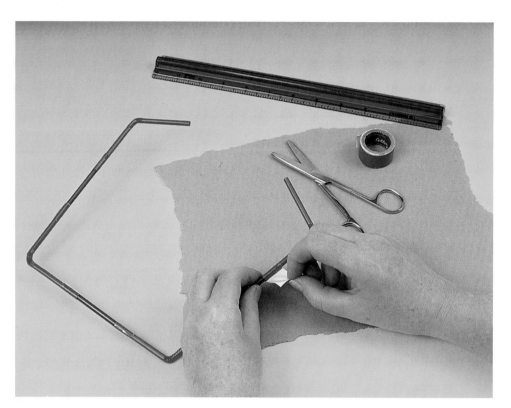

6 Repeat this process, joining together four red and three blue straws, as shown.

7 Cut 3in from each of the two long blue straw ends on the main piece (see picture **4**). Now join the main piece to the neck piece you have just made. (Do this by making ½in slits in the straws, as before.)

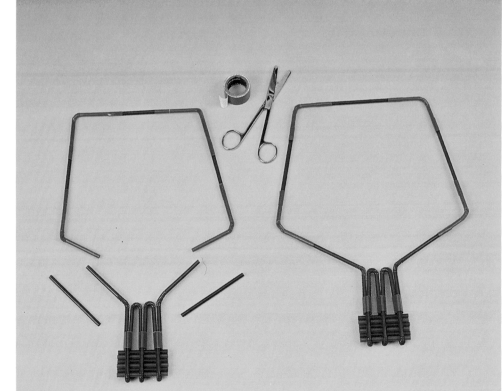

8 Wrap a short length of masking tape around the quill of a feather until it is a good fit when slotted inside a straw.

9 Put glue in the ends of the red straws that lie across the bottom section of the necklace, and push a taped feather into each. Three more feathers can be inserted into the blue straws. Try arranging the straws in different ways, and use different colors. Color white chicken, duck and gull feathers with inks to make your own designs.

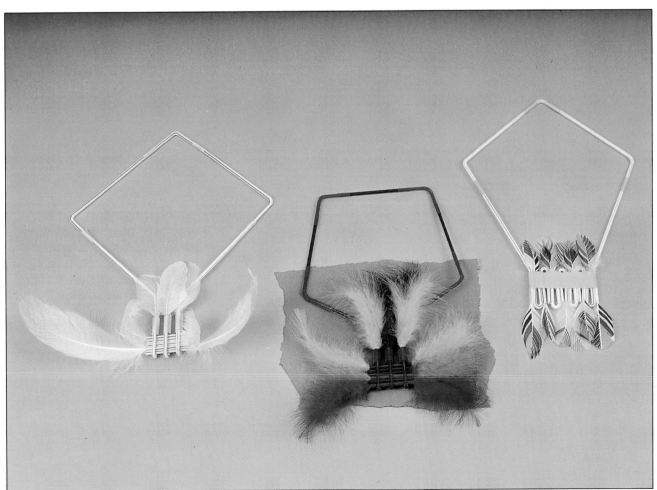

Acetate bracelet

Thin strips of colored acetate held together by eyelets are the basis for this design, which bends to fit many wrist sizes. It is also possible to make the bracelet from other flexible material such as thick colored paper or strips of plastic food packaging.

You will need cardboard, a ruler, a pencil, scissors, a ¼in hole punch, four sheets of colored acetate (red, blue, green and yellow, 0.175mm thick), ten eyelets for a ¼in hole, an eyelet punch and masking tape.

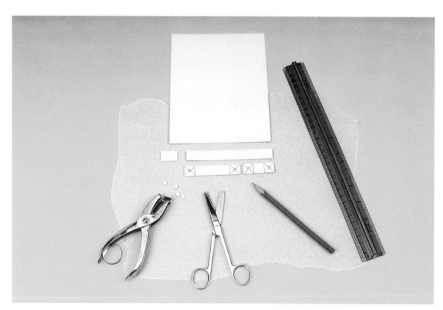

1 Cut a strip of cardboard ¾in wide, then cut off two pieces, one 1¾in in length, the other 3in. Construct a square at each end of each piece of cardboard. Draw diagonal lines in the squares, then use the hole punch to punch out a hole in each square, at the point where the diagonal lines cross. Use these pieces of cardboard as patterns.

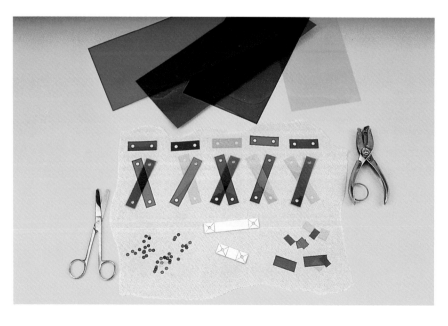

2 Cut ten long (3in) and five short (1¾in) strips of acetate. Punch holes in each end of each strip, using the patterns as a guide. (If you use the colors shown in the picture, assembling the strips will be easier to follow.)

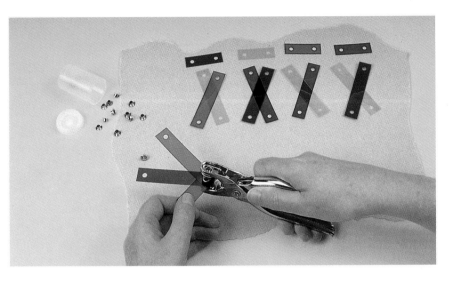

3 Take two long strips and one short strip. Place the short strip between the long ones, lining up the holes. Insert an eyelet and rivet the strips together with the eyelet punch.

4 Take two more long strips and rivet them at the other end of the short strip. Position the short strip between the long strips, as before.

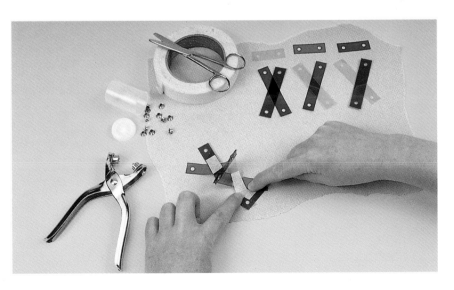

5 Arrange the long strips to form two crosses. Look at picture **4**. One cross is made with the red and green strips, on the right. The other is made with the green and yellow strips, on the left. The angle of each cross should let the holes in the ends line up with the holes in another short strip. Tape the crossed strips together to hold them in position.

6 Add two more long strips to the assembly, riveting one to each end of the short strip added at the base of one of the crosses. (Catch in the ends of the cross, too, sandwiching the short strip between the long strips as before.)

7 Repeat the process described in pictures **5** and **6** until you have used up all the strips. (Make sure that the short strips are always sandwiched between the long strips.) Join the two ends together to complete the bracelet.

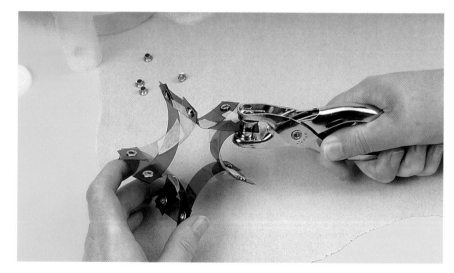

8 Remove all the pieces of masking tape and cut off any sharp corners.

9 You can decorate this bracelet by threading tape, braid or ribbon through the eyelets. Now experiment with other flexible materials.

Decorated egg

The "bejeweled" egg shown here is designed in the style of the Faberge eggs that were given as Easter presents by the Czar of Russia's family at the beginning of this century. These eggs were made of gold, silver and enamel and were decorated with precious jewels. This design is based on something rather less costly – a hen's egg!

You will need a bowl, an egg, a broach-tipped bradawl, a knitting needle (no.11), gold enamel paint, a paintbrush, an egg cup, UHU (or similar adhesive), four birthday cake candle holders, gold lurex braid (¼in wide flat strip), scissors, a rhinestone strip (3mm wide), a pearl bead (approximately 10mm diameter) and rhinestones (¼in diameter, twelve red and seven blue).

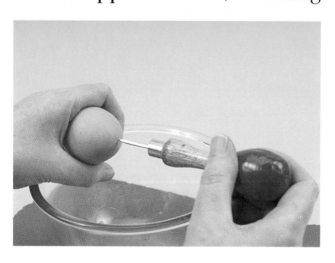

1 Wash and dry the egg. Work over the bowl in case the egg breaks. Take the egg in one hand and hold it gently but firmly around the middle. Make a hole in the pointed end of the egg by gently pressing the broach tip of the bradawl against the egg while rotating it.

2 Keep turning when you break through the shell, until you have opened up a hole about ¼in in diameter. Make another hole at the opposite end of the egg.

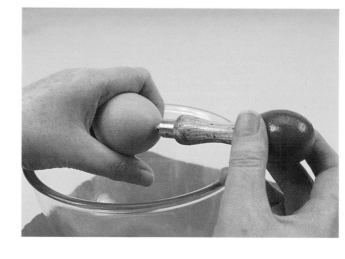

3 Hold the egg over the bowl and blow through one hole so that the contents come out through the other. (The contents can be used for cooking if everything is kept clean.) When you have emptied the shell, carefully wash and dry it.

4 Support the eggshell on the knitting needle and paint the shell gold. Leave to dry.

5 Rest the egg in the egg cup, pointed end down. Place small blobs of glue on the petals of three of the candle holders and attach these around the hole at the fat end of the egg, as shown. Leave to dry.

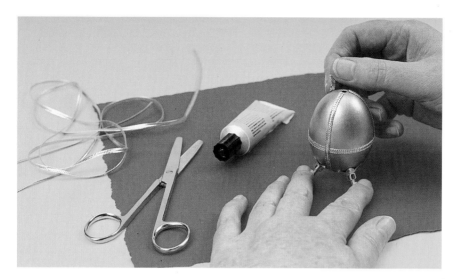

6 When the glue is dry, take the egg out of the egg cup and stand it on its candle-holder legs. Cut a length of gold braid to fit around the middle of the egg and glue in position. Glue three more lengths from between the legs to just short of the top hole.

7 Cut three lengths of rhinestone strip to fit from the legs to just short of the top hole. Glue these in position (one strip should run from each leg). Cut more pieces of rhinestone strip to fit above the gold braid around the middle. Glue short lengths around the feet.

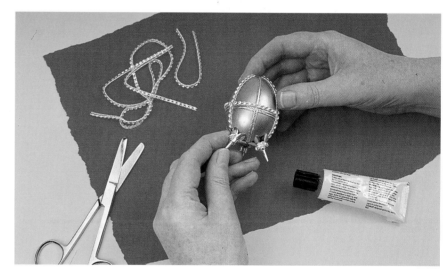

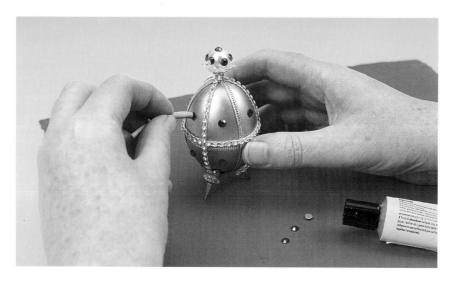

8 Glue the pearl bead into the last candle holder. Decorate it by gluing on blue rhinestone "sapphires" using one to cover the hole in the bead. Glue the candle holder into the hole in the top of the egg. Glue red rhinestone "rubies" into the panels, as shown.

9 Use different colors of enamel paint, and try using buttons, beads and cake decorations to help create all kinds of exotic eggs.

Sources of tools and materials

Most craft items used in this book can be obtained from stationers and/or artists' materials stores. Fabric stores stock eyelets and eyelet punches, embroidery thread, rhinestones, gold braid and scissors. Supermarkets stock straws, cake decorations and aluminum foil, as well as rolling pins. Home centers and pet shops that sell aquariums stock clear plastic tubing. Garden centers stock plastic-coated wire. Hardware stores and craft stores stock pliers, wire cutters, round-nosed pliers, bradawls and colored adhesive tapes. Water pipe insulating foam can be obtained at plumbing supply stores and home centers.

Beads, glass stones, rhinestones, gold braid, embroidery thread and feathers can be bought from craft and fabric stores.

Some helpful books

Davidson, Ian. *Ideas for Jewelry.* New York; Watson-Guptill, 1973.

Lerner, Sharon. *Making Jewelry.* Minneapolis; Lerner, 1977.

Mosesson, Gloria R. *Jewelry Craft for Beginners.* Indianapolis; Bobbs-Merrill, 1975.

Rodway, Avril. *Step by Step Guide to Jewelry Making.* New York; Hamlyn, 1973.

Sanford, William Robert. *Jewelry: Queen of Crafts.* New York; Bruce Pub. Co., 1970.

Sommer, Elyse. *Wearable Crafts: Creating Clothing, Body Adornments, and Jewelry from Fabrics and Fibers.* New York; Crown, 1976.

Zechlin, Katharina. *Creative Enameling and Jewelry-Making.* New York; Sterling Pub., 1965.

Jewelry can be traced back some 7,000 years to the earliest known civilizations in Mesopotamia and Egypt, and is found in some form or other in every society that has existed since, from the most primitive to the most civilized.

A study of a society's jewelry, often leads us to a better understanding of that society. Seafaring societies, for example, made jewelry in the form of objects such as boats and fish. These items, known as amulets, were thought to have power. They could bring good luck or provide protection from storms.

On an individual level, jewelry can show how important a person is. Think, for example, of a queen and her crown, or a millionaire and his or her gold watch. Think of the chief of a so-called "primitive" society, and his headdress of rare feathers. Jewelry does not have to be made of precious materials. The very first type of jewelry was probably made of pebbles and shells. Later, iron, copper and bronze were used.

But the images of luxury and glamor conjured up by jewelry made from precious metals or stones are difficult to dismiss. Substitutes have therefore been developed for many valuable and rare materials so that those people who cannot afford the "real thing" can still wear similar products. As long ago as 1740, a Frenchman called Georges-Frederic Strass perfected a way of making imitation diamonds and other precious stones from cut glass. His discovery transformed the jewelry of the time, and encouraged the development of "costume" jewelry.

In an attempt to identify the real from the fake, marks have been used since Roman times to indicate the quality of metals. These are known as hallmarks.

Jewelry styles change to suit public taste. Egyptian-style jewelry became popular during the 1920s and 1930s, when there was great public excitement over the excavation of the Pharaohs' tombs in Egypt.

Today, as throughout history, jewelry is worn as a sign of status and wealth, to protect and bring luck, and as a way of expressing one's personality.

PRINTED IN BELGIUM BY

INTERNATIONAL BOOK PRODUCTION